Merry Christmas S0-DZC-285

fine young grandson. We
hope you enjoy the book
about the farm animals God made!
Grandma Ville & Grandpa Francis
Swearingen

God Made FARM ANIMALS

written by Sue Turner Hayes
photography by Robert Cushman Hayes

Library of Congress Catalog Card No. 83-051628
©1984. The STANDARD PUBLISHING Company, Cincinnati, Ohio
Division of STANDEX INTERNATIONAL Corporation. Printed in U.S.A.

We'll visit a farm
And there we will see,
The animals God made
For you and for me.

The gentle brown cow
Greets us with a moo.
Perhaps she is saying,
"Well, how do you do?"

Here is a pony
To ride when we play.
When he gets hungry
The farmer gives him hay.

The farmer's alarm clock
Is not by his bed.
It's the cock-a-doodle-do
Of a rooster named Fred.

Who's lazy and fat
And just loves to dig?
The answer is easy.
It's the farmer's pink pig.

We see a squirrel
Hiding nuts in the ground.
In winter he'll eat
All the nuts he has found.

Here is the kitten
Who sleeps in the hay.
Her job is to keep
All the mice away.

This hen's smooth feathers
Are pure snowy white.
We feed her grain and
She clucks with delight.

The baby raccoon's
In a tree, oh, so tall.
He hangs from a limb,
But we don't think he'll fall.

We must look quickly
To see the baby deer.
This fawn will run away
If we try to come near.

This deer lives
In the woods near the farm.
God makes him swift
To keep him from harm.

When we walk in the garden,
It's all warm and sunny.
We look in the lettuce
And see a white bunny.

The farmer's best friend
Is always by his side.
His dog on the tractor
Is waiting for a ride.

This baby goat
Likes to be fed.
We'll feed him and pet him
On his knobby head.

This goat looks so funny
With horns on his head.
They say he'll eat cans,
Or anything he's fed.

Here are the geese
Who honk when they talk.
This goose mom and dad
Take their babies for a walk.

If a farm duck gets hot,
He knows which road to take.
He waddles on down
And jumps in the lake.

Here is a woolly sheep
Waiting patiently.
We'll give his soft head a pat,
And go on merrily.

God gave this burro
Such big floppy ears.
He looks so funny—
We wonder what he hears.

Who leaves her cocoon
And takes to the sky?
Then sits on a flower—
This butterfly!

The robin has babies
In a tree up so high.
She'll feed them and love them
And teach them to fly.

Visiting the farm
Is sure lots of fun.
We go to the meadow
To see horses run.

It's time to leave
All the animals we see!
The farm animals God made,
For you and for me.